This journal belongs to

Ren Stengel

Date

May 27, 2021

Living a Life I LOVE journal

Ellie Claire
Hachette Book Group
1290 Avenue of the Americas, New York, NY 10104
ellieclaire.com

First Edition: LeatherLuxe® (March 2020)

Ellie Claire is a division of Hachette Book Group, Inc.
The Ellie Claire name and logo are trademarks of Hachette Book Group, Inc.
The publisher is not responsible for websites (or their content) that are not owned by the publisher.

Unless otherwise noted, the quotes in this book were taken from Joyce Meyer's book *Living a Life I Love*.

Print book interior design by Bart Dawson.

ISBN: 9781546033691

Printed in China
RRD-S
10 9 8 7 6 5 4 3 2 1

He will never leave you or forsake you.

He will guide your steps.

EMBRACE
the adventure of
BEING LED
by the Spirit!

Your plan may be good, but God's plan is great.
Your plan may bring *some* happiness,
but God's plan brings overflowing joy.

We know [with great confidence] that God [who is deeply concerned about us] causes all things to work together [as a plan] for good for those who love God.

Romans 8:28 AMP

If we will simply trust God and submit to His plan, there is no enemy or obstacle that can keep God's purposes from coming to pass.

God-of-the-Angel-Armies has planned it. Who could ever cancel such plans?
His is the hand that's reached out. Who could brush it aside?

Isaiah 14:27 MSG

When you realize God is in control, it takes all the pressure off. You don't have to worry or fret.... You can simply rest in the fact that God has it all planned out.

Instead of worrying, pray.... Before you know it, a sense of God's wholeness, everything coming together for good, will come and settle you down.

PHILIPPIANS 4:6–7 MSG

We can embrace the great adventure of being led by the Holy Spirit and trust that He will lead us day by day into the perfect plan our Father has for us.

For those who are led by the Spirit of God are the children of God.

Romans 8:14 niv

God's plan is for you to be redeemed from sin and guilt, made right with Him, and have peace in your soul.... But God's plan goes beyond the inner life. [He] wants you to enjoy your life every day.

I came that they may have and *enjoy life, and have it in abundance [to the full, till it overflows].*

John 10:10 AMP

God's plan...will always be something that fulfills
the very desires He has placed in your heart.
And it is guaranteed to be something far greater than
what you could have imagined on your own.

Take delight in the Lord,
and he will give you your heart's desires.
Psalm 37:4 NLT

God's plan in your life doesn't happen overnight—
it's a process. He is building your faith,
healing your soul, refreshing your spirit all in due time.

He who began a good work in you will carry it on
to completion until the day of Christ Jesus.

PHILIPPIANS 1:6 NIV

The obligations of daily living don't have to steal your joy....
It's all about choosing to see the blessings
of God and the good in each day.

This…is the day the Lord has made; let us rejoice and be glad in it.

Psalm 118:24 AMP

When we become people who love others
around us on a daily basis,
our lives are tremendously enriched.

I have told you this so that my joy may be in you and that your joy may be complete. My command is this: Love each other as I have loved you.

John 15:11–12 niv

It is amazing to me that even in the midst of running the universe, God still has us on His mind.... Just think about it—*God has you on His mind all of the time!*

How precious also are Your thoughts to me, O God!
How vast is the sum of them!
If I could count them, they would outnumber the sand.

PSALM 139:17–18 AMP

One of God's greatest gifts to us is that He enables us by His grace to enjoy life even in the midst of trouble and difficulty.

Our hearts ache, but we always have joy. We are poor, but we give spiritual riches to others. We own nothing, and yet we have everything.

2 Corinthians 6:10 NLT

It's important to God that you rejoice each day, because He knows how powerfully it will affect your life.

Rejoice in the Lord always [delight, take pleasure in Him];
again I will say, rejoice!

PHILIPPIANS 4:4 AMP

You cannot swim for new horizons until you have courage to lose sight of the shore.

WILLIAM FAULKNER

Trust God from the bottom of your heart; don't try to figure out everything on your own. Listen for God's voice in everything you do, everywhere you go; he's the one who will keep you on track.

Proverbs 3:5–6 msg

We are not created by God to shrink back in fear,
but to boldly go forward as we trust Him
to never leave us or forsake us.

For God has not given us a spirit of fear and timidity,
but of power, love, and self-discipline.

2 Timothy 1:7 NLT

Focusing on God's promises instead of the world's problems is the best way to overcome fear.

Fear not, for I am with you; be not dismayed, for I am your God. I will strengthen you, yes, I will help you, I will uphold you with My righteous right hand.

ISAIAH 41:10 NKJV

If you'll stand on the promises of God's Word and move forward in faith, you'll be amazed at the joy that comes with moving past your fears.

When I am afraid, I will put my trust and *faith in You.*

Psalm 56:3 AMP

Grace is the power of God that enables us to do with ease what we could never do on our own.

By grace you have been saved through faith, and that not of yourselves; it is the gift of God, not of works, lest anyone should boast.

Ephesians 2:8–9 NKJV

God has called us to enter His rest. He does not want us to be frustrated, but instead He desires that we enjoy peace.

Come to me, all of you who are weary and carry heavy burdens,
and I will give you rest.

MATTHEW 11:28 NLT

In the midst of all the challenges and surprises of life, there is good news: We have a way to be happy when circumstances don't necessarily suit us.... And that way is the grace of God!

I have learned the secret of being content in any and every situation,
whether well fed or hungry, whether living in plenty or in want.
I can do all this through him who gives me strength.

PHILIPPIANS 4:12–13 NIV

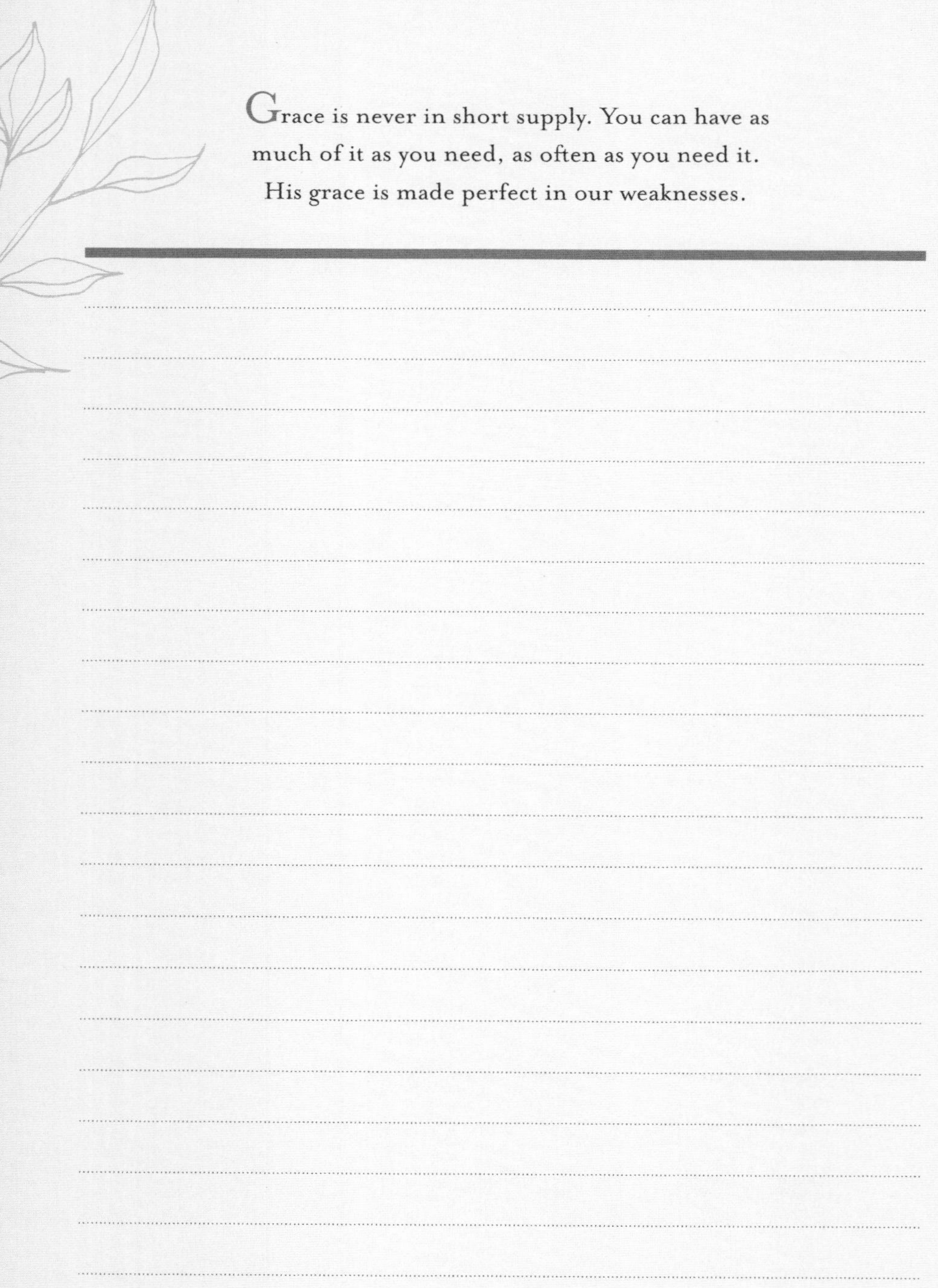

Grace is never in short supply. You can have as much of it as you need, as often as you need it. His grace is made perfect in our weaknesses.

My grace is sufficient for you, for My strength is made perfect in weakness.

2 Corinthians 12:9 NKJV

No matter what you did in the past, or what someone did to you, you are more than your past pain. You belong to God and He has a good plan for you.

Do not conform to the pattern of this world, but be transformed by the renewing of your mind. Then you will be able to test and approve what God's will is—his good, pleasing and perfect will.

~ROMANS 12:2 NIV

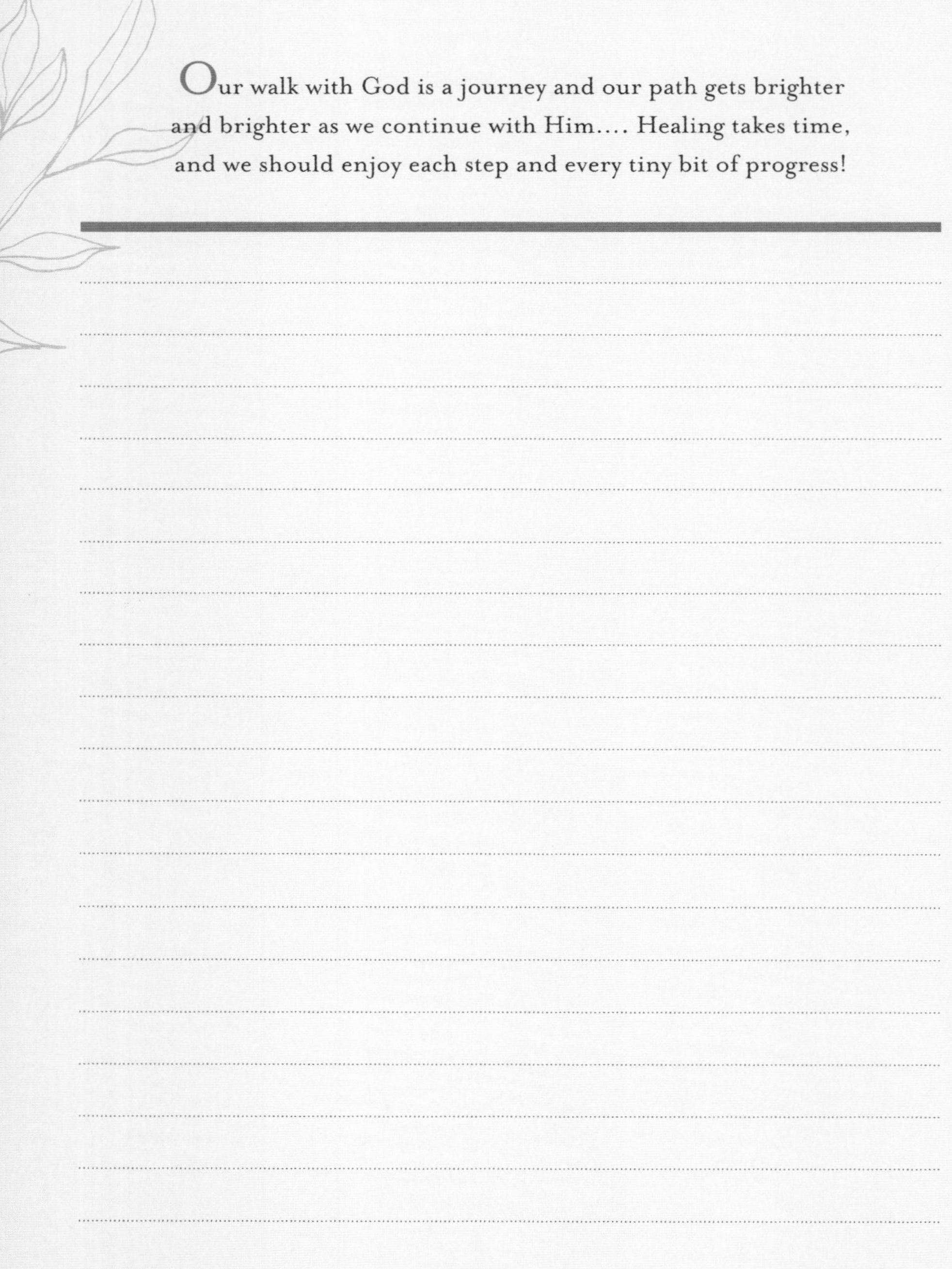

Our walk with God is a journey and our path gets brighter and brighter as we continue with Him.... Healing takes time, and we should enjoy each step and every tiny bit of progress!

May the Master take you by the hand and lead you along the path of God's love and Christ's endurance.

2 THESSALONIANS 3:5 MSG

God is concerned about everything that concerns you,
and don't ever think that He is too busy to help you.
What we may see as a dead end, God sees as a new beginning!

Let's not get tired of doing what is good. At just the right time we will reap a harvest of blessing if we don't give up.

Galatians 6:9 NLT

Our hope is not limited by what we can see around us or what we went through previously. Hope that sustains us is hope that is based on the Word of God and His promises for our lives.

Do not dwell on the past. See, I am doing a new thing!
Now it springs up; do you not perceive it? I am making a way
in the wilderness and streams in the wasteland.

Isaiah 43:18–19 NIV

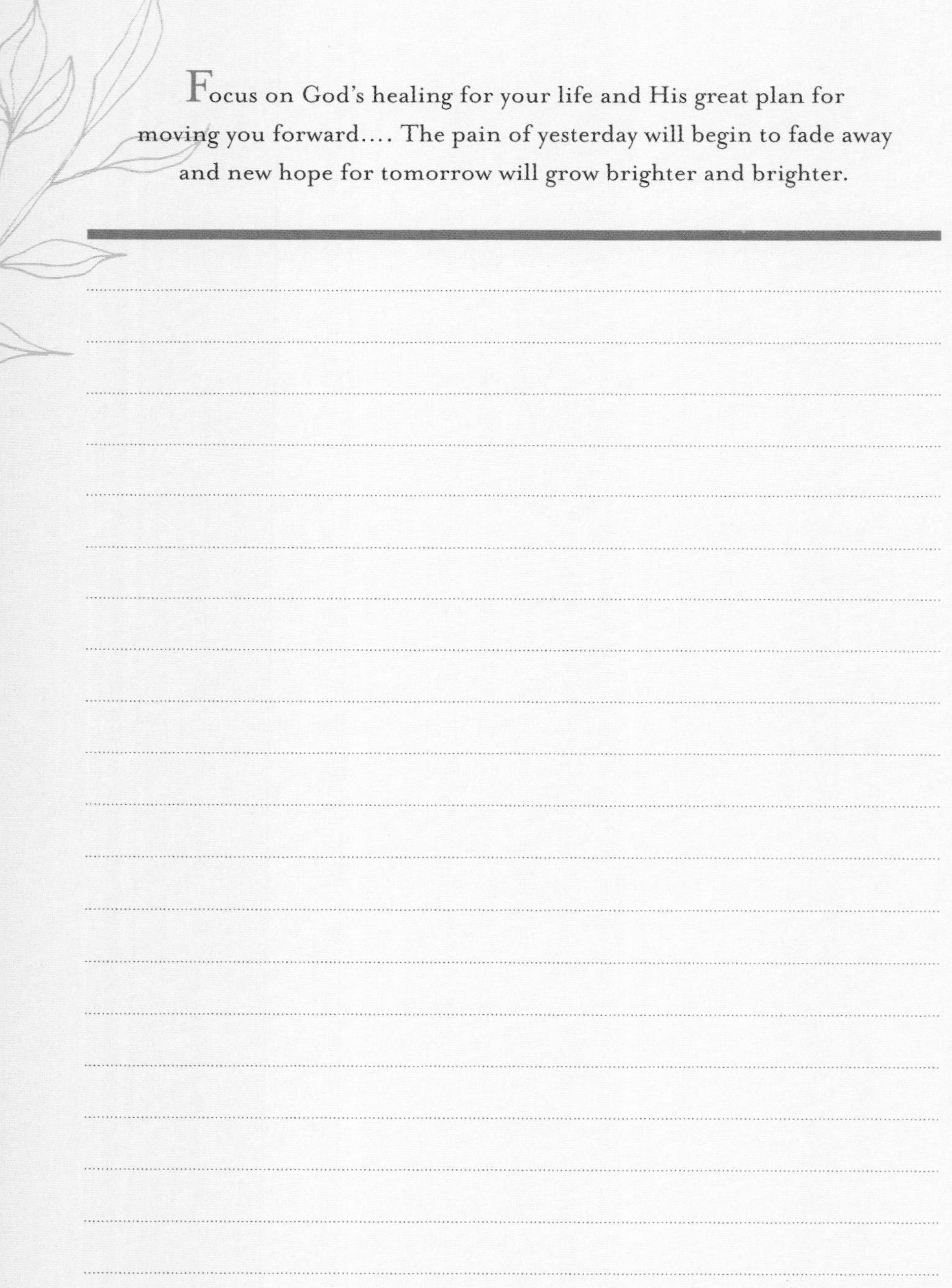

Focus on God's healing for your life and His great plan for moving you forward.... The pain of yesterday will begin to fade away and new hope for tomorrow will grow brighter and brighter.

Praise be to the God and Father of our Lord Jesus Christ! In his great mercy he has given us new birth into a living hope through the resurrection of Jesus Christ.

1 PETER 1:3 NIV

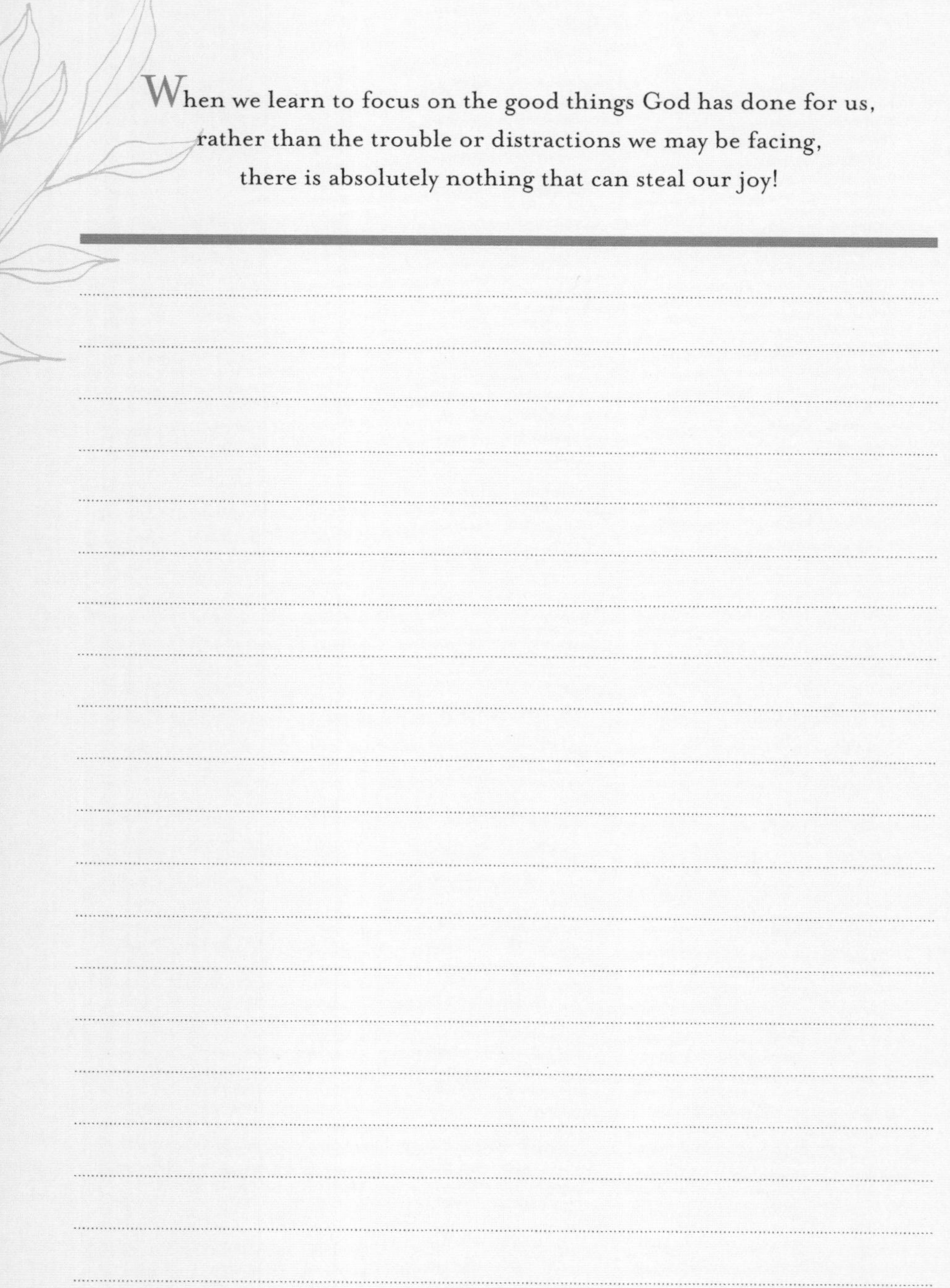

When we learn to focus on the good things God has done for us, rather than the trouble or distractions we may be facing, there is absolutely nothing that can steal our joy!

Every good and perfect gift is from above, coming down from the Father of the heavenly lights, who does not change like shifting shadows.

James 1:17 NIV

Peace and joy can be found in the ordinary, inexpensive, overlooked things in life, like a walk or a laugh. It's a wonderful thought: Contentment is often found in the small stuff.

A devout life does bring wealth, but it's the rich simplicity of being yourself before God. Since we entered the world penniless and will leave it penniless, if we have bread on the table and shoes on our feet, that's enough.

1 Timothy 6:6–8 msg

The idea of counting our blessings isn't so we can stockpile benefits for ourselves...it's so we can share those blessings with others.... Generosity is the key to happiness!

The generous will prosper; those who refresh others will themselves be refreshed.

PROVERBS 11:25 NLT

God loves you so much that He lavishly pours out His goodness, His peace, His joy, and His blessings on your life. Never forget that. You are loaded down with blessings from heaven.

See what great love the Father has lavished on us, that we should be called children of God! And that is what we are!

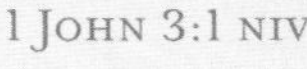

1 JOHN 3:1 NIV

Let me encourage you to relax. All that pressure, all that striving to be perfect, all of those self-imposed expectations—take a break and let God help.

Steep your life in God-reality, God-initiative, God-provisions. Don't worry about missing out. You'll find all your everyday human concerns will be met.

MATTHEW 6:33 MSG

You are complete, beautiful, whole, and accepted in Christ....
We are daily becoming what we already are in Christ!

The Spirit himself testifies with our spirit that we are God's children.
Now if we are children, then we are heirs—heirs of God and co-heirs with Christ.

Romans 8:16–17 niv

When you begin to agree with God about who you are and the future God has for you, there is no way you can't love your life. It's all about perspective.

If you're serious about living this new resurrection life with Christ, act *like it….*
Look up, and be alert to what is going on around Christ—
that's where the action is. See things from his *perspective.*

Colossians 3:1–2 msg

God doesn't need to rest, but He did it to give us an example of how we should live. If God rested...we should too.

By the seventh day God completed His work which He had done,
and He rested (ceased) on the seventh day from all His work which He had done.

GENESIS 2:2 AMP

The right attitude can make any situation better.
It doesn't really matter what is happening on the outside…
what matters is what is happening on the inside.

Do everything without grumbling or arguing, so that you may become blameless and pure.... Then you will shine among them like stars in the sky

PHILIPPIANS 2:14 NIV

Hope is a powerful and life-enriching gift from God.

"For I know the plans and *thoughts that I have for you," says the* L*ORD*, *"plans for peace* and *well-being and not for disaster, to give you a future and a hope."*

JEREMIAH 29:11 AMP

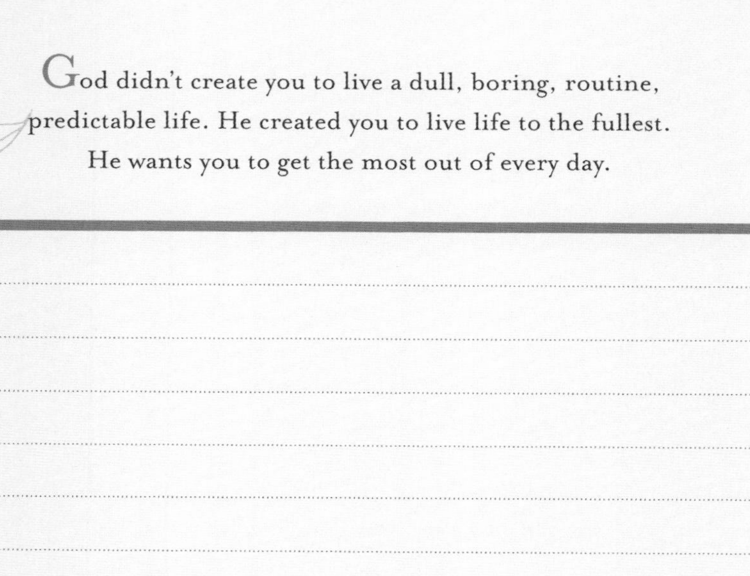

God didn't create you to live a dull, boring, routine, predictable life. He created you to live life to the fullest. He wants you to get the most out of every day.

As it is written: "What no eye has seen, what no ear has heard, and what no human mind has conceived"—the things God has prepared for those who love him."

1 Corinthians 2:9 niv

What you have is more than enough. God has already provided what you need to live a refreshing, routine-shattering life!

I have learned to be content [and self-sufficient through Christ, satisfied to the point where I am not disturbed or uneasy] regardless of my circumstances.

PHILIPPIANS 4:11 AMP

You've been given so much from God....
Your resources, your time schedule, your gifts and talents—
God can do something incredible with it all.

God can do anything, you know—far more than you could ever imagine or guess or request in your wildest dreams! He does it not by pushing us around but by working within us, his Spirit deeply and gently within us.

Ephesians 3:20–21 msg

In whatever season you are in, God wants you to know that you can find peace and contentment.

Whatever you do [whatever your task may be], work from the soul [that is, put in your very best effort], as [something done] for the Lord and not for men.

Colossians 3:23 AMP

True promotion comes from God. Your times are in His hands, and you can be content while you wait for change.

So be content with who you are, and don't put on airs.
God's strong hand is on you; he'll promote you at the right time.
Live carefree before God; he is most careful with you.

1 PETER 5:6–7 MSG

Jesus gives us *His* peace—not as the world gives, but His own special peace. His peace functions *in* the storms of life rather than waiting until... life is bright and sunny once again.

Peace I leave with you, My peace I give to you; not as the world gives do I give to you. Let not your heart be troubled, neither let it be afraid.

JOHN 14:27 NKJV

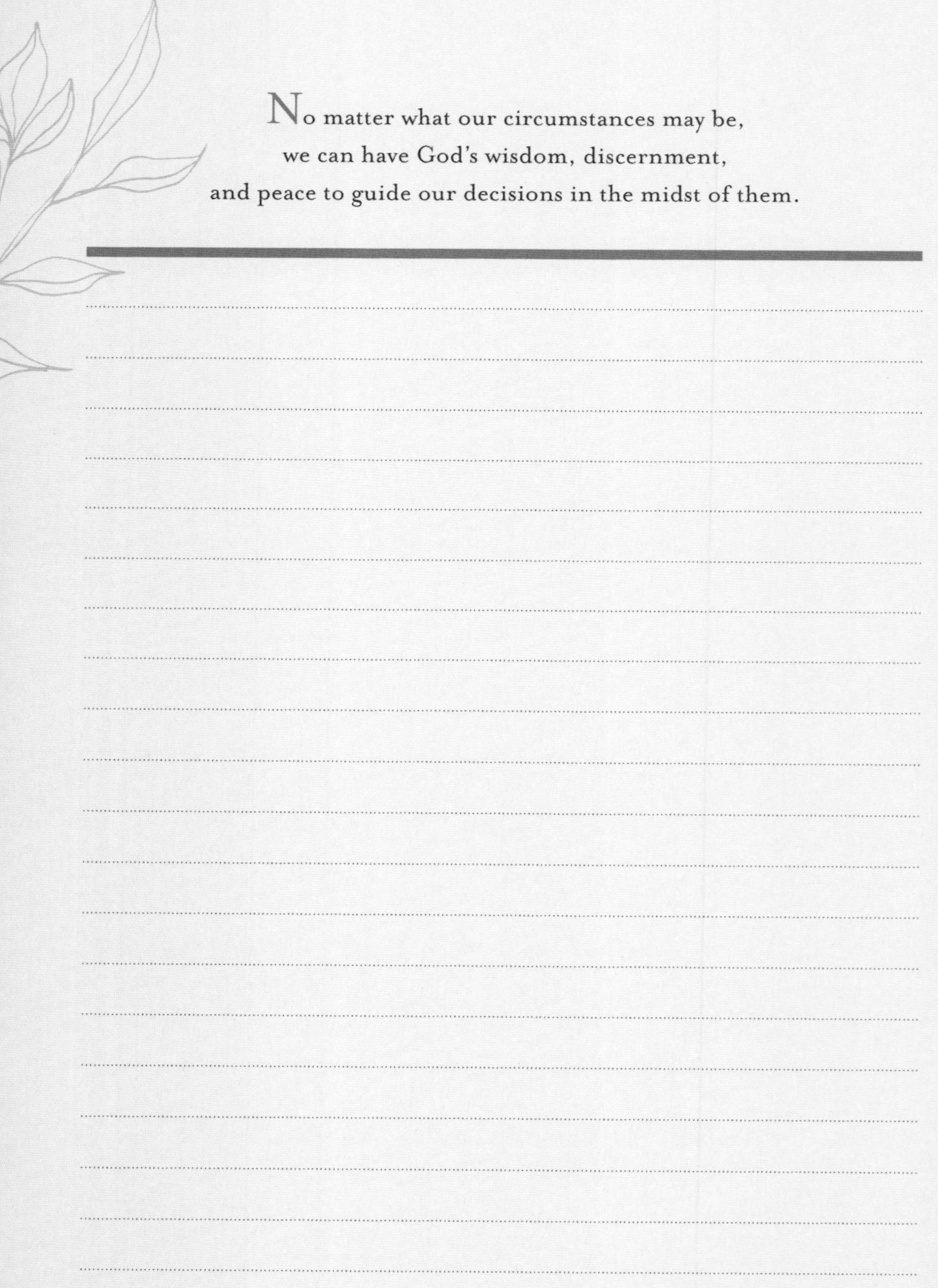

No matter what our circumstances may be,
we can have God's wisdom, discernment,
and peace to guide our decisions in the midst of them.

When He, the Spirit of Truth, comes, He will guide you into all the truth [full and complete truth].

John 16:13 amp

Peaceful thoughts turn into a peaceful life! [Spend] time each day reading and meditating on the Word of God. Then pray and ask Him to help you...apply the wisdom you discover to your everyday life.

Whatever is true, whatever is noble, whatever is right, whatever is pure, whatever is lovely, whatever is admirable—if anything is excellent or praiseworthy—think about such things.

PHILIPPIANS 4:8 NIV

Every new day in Christ is a new opportunity for something incredible to happen.

It is because of the LORD's lovingkindnesses that we are not consumed, because His [tender] compassions never fail. They are new every morning; great and *beyond measure is Your faithfulness.*

LAMENTATIONS 3:22–23 AMP

Embrace your opportunity and do something courageous today in that spirit of power and love.

Be strong and courageous! Do not be afraid or discouraged.
For the Lord *your God is with you wherever you go.*

Joshua 1:9 NLT

Cherish your yesterdays, dream your tomorrows, and live your todays.

Anonymous

Don't worry about anything; instead, pray about everything. Tell God what you need, and thank him for all he has done. Then you will experience God's peace, which exceeds anything we can understand.

PHILIPPIANS 4:6–7 NLT

Live every day like it's your last. Start doing the things that are important to you, and things that you enjoy.

Teach us to number our days, that we may gain a heart of wisdom.

PSALM 90:12 NIV

God gave us the capacity to laugh....
Laughter brings health to the soul...and the body.

A happy heart is good medicine and *a joyful mind causes healing.*

Proverbs 17:22 amp

Your greatest joy definitely comes from doing something for another, especially when it was done with no thought of something in return.

John Wooden

The generous will prosper; those who refresh others will themselves be refreshed.

PROVERBS 11:25 NLT

What lies behind us and what lies before us are tiny matters compared to what lies within us.

Ralph Waldo Emerson

Cultivate inner beauty, the gentle, gracious kind that God delights in.

1 Peter 3:4 MSG

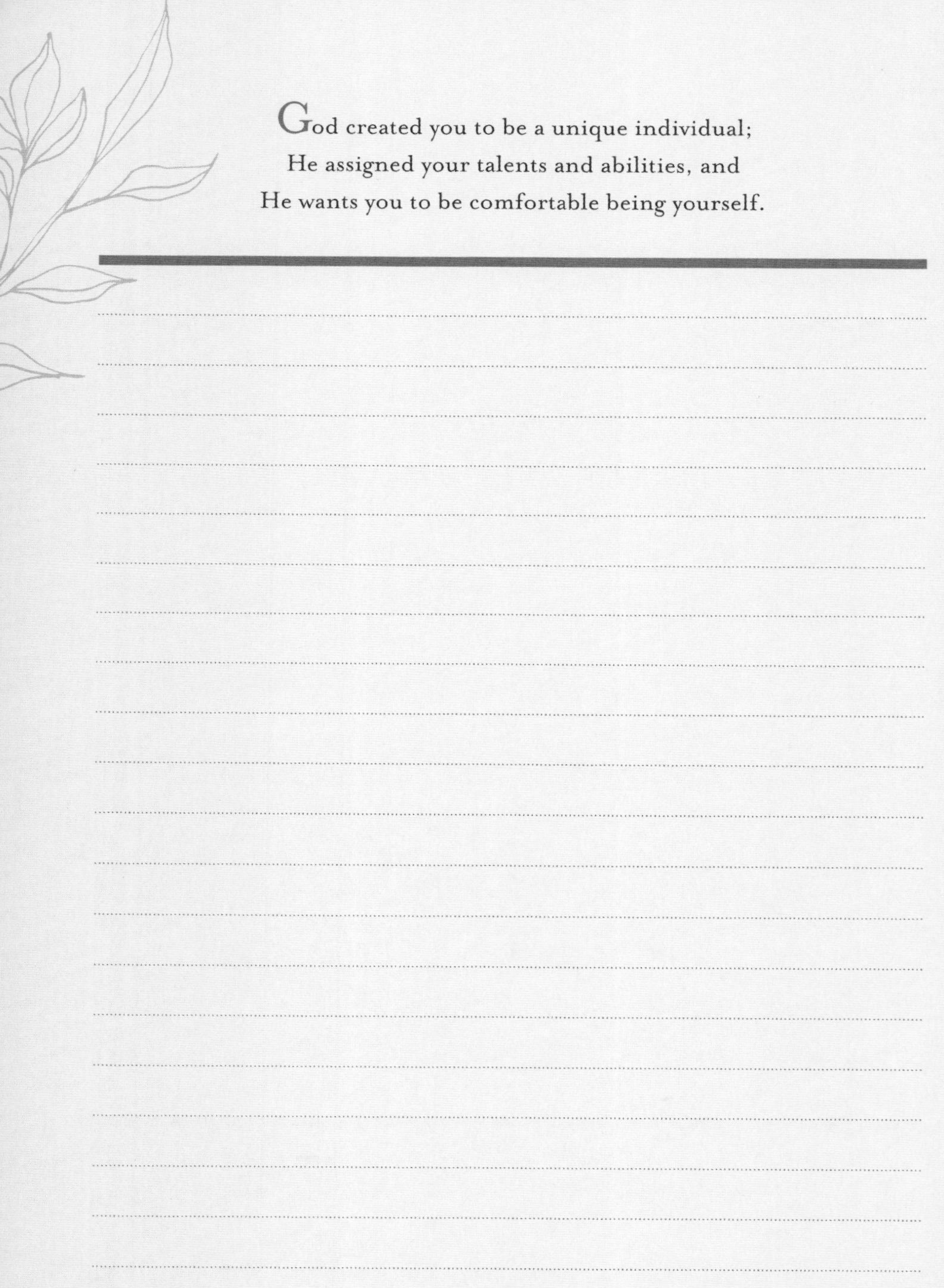

God created you to be a unique individual;
He assigned your talents and abilities, and
He wants you to be comfortable being yourself.

You formed my innermost parts; you knit me [together] in my mother's womb.

Psalm 139:13 AMP

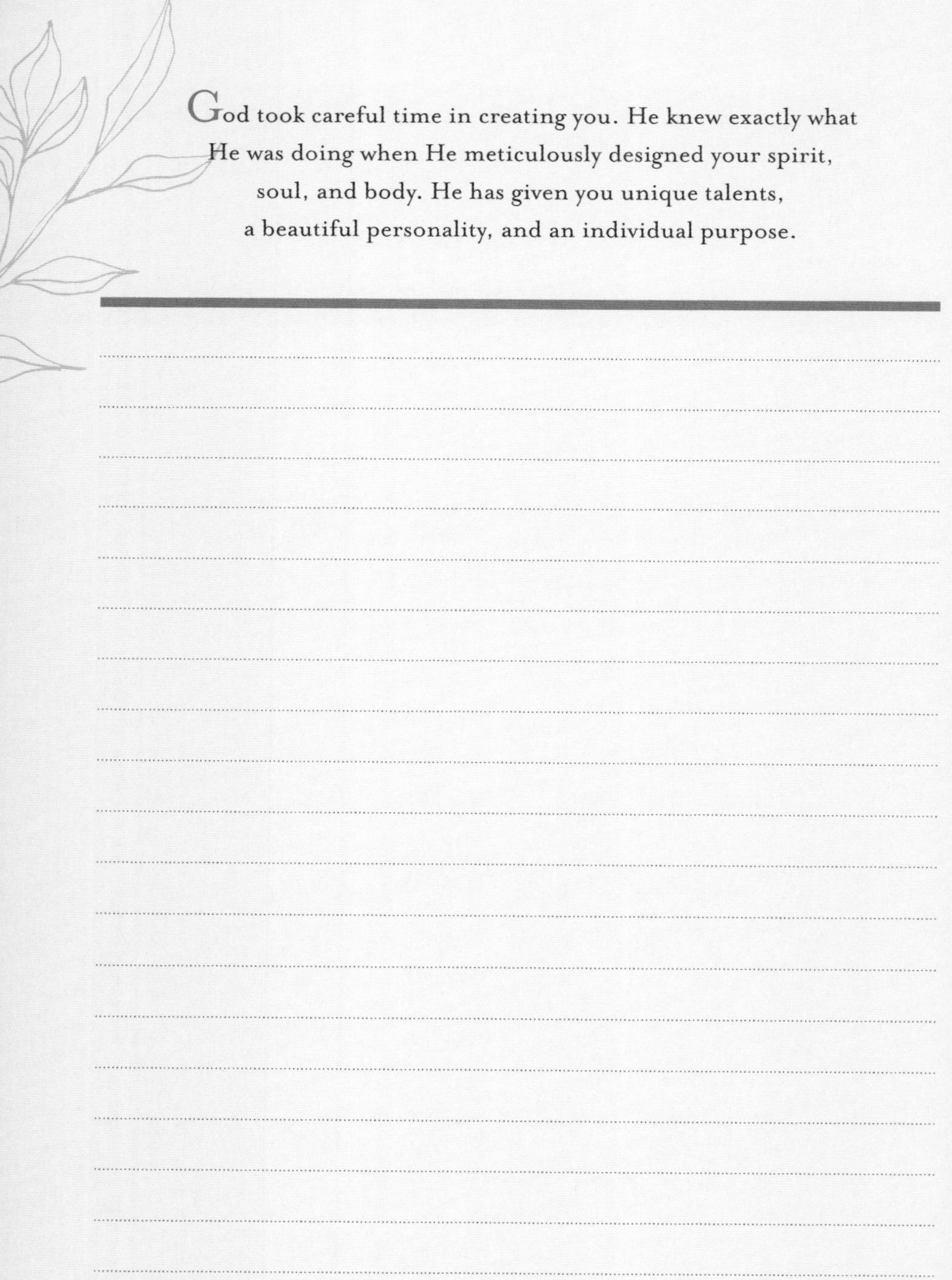

God took careful time in creating you. He knew exactly what He was doing when He meticulously designed your spirit, soul, and body. He has given you unique talents, a beautiful personality, and an individual purpose.

I will give thanks and *praise to You, for I am fearfully and wonderfully made; wonderful are Your works, and my soul knows it very well.*

PSALM 139:14 AMP

God wants us to find our worth and value in the fact that we were created by Him, we belong to Him, He loves us, and He has a very good plan for our lives.

Long before he laid down earth's foundations, he had us in mind, had settled on us as the focus of his love, to be made whole and holy by his love.

Ephesians 1:4 msg

The key to living that secure life...is knowing who you were created to be, receiving God's unconditional love for you, and basing your worth on what the Word of God says about you, rather than anything else.

This [peace, righteousness, security, and triumph over opposition] is the heritage of the servants of the Lord.

Isaiah 54:17 AMP

God not only sees what we are at this moment, but He sees what we are becoming. He sees the end from the beginning.

I make known the end from the beginning, from ancient times, what is still to come.

Isaiah 46:10 NIV

The greatest theological insight that I have ever had is this: Jesus loves me, this I know, for the Bible tells me so.

KARL BARTH

For God so loved the world that He gave His only begotten Son,
that whoever believes in Him should not perish but have everlasting life.

John 3:16 NKJV

We often try to exist on information alone, but what we truly need is revelation...about the love that God has for us and to be rooted deeply in it.

Then Christ will make his home in your hearts as you trust in him. Your roots will grow down into God's love and keep you strong.

EPHESIANS 3:17 NLT

My worth and value are found in the truth that I am a child of God, not in what I do, what I have, what I look like, or what others think about me.

If God gives such attention to the appearance of wildflowers—
most of which are never even seen—don't you think he'll attend to you,
take pride in you, do his best for you?

Matthew 6:30 msg

When you grasp that God loves you unconditionally, simply for who you are, you will be free to love your life and enjoy the person He has created you to be.

May you have the power to understand, as all God's people should, how wide, how long, how high, and how deep his love is.

EPHESIANS 3:18 NLT

If everything is the same, then nothing stands out and shines. It is God's infinite variety combined together that creates amazing beauty.

God's various gifts are handed out everywhere; but they all originate in God's Spirit....
All kinds of things are handed out by the Spirit, and to all kinds of people!
The variety is wonderful.

1 Corinthians 12:4, 7 msg

Love is what makes the ride worthwhile.

Franklin P. Jones

Love from the center of who you are; don't fake it. Run for dear life from evil; hold on for dear life to good. Be good friends who love deeply.

ROMANS 12:9–10 MSG

God is love.... When you make love the focus of your life, you're making God the number one priority in your life.

Dear friends, let us continue to love one another, for love comes from God. Anyone who loves is a child of God and knows God.

1 John 4:7 NLT

It's like someone turns on the light in a dark room.
We begin to see things we could never see before.
Love always drives away the darkness.

You were once darkness, but now you are light in the Lord. Live as children of light.

EPHESIANS 5:8 NIV

Showing love to other people will become a complete joy!... This is a great spiritual secret, and when we do it, it adds tremendous spiritual power to our lives.

I want you woven into a tapestry of love, in touch with everything there is to know of God. Then you will have minds confident and at rest, focused on Christ, God's great mystery.

Colossians 2:2 msg

There is no better influence for your life than the Word of God—it is filled with His promises, instructions, and assurances of love for you.

Whatever was written in earlier times was written for our instruction, so that through endurance and the encouragement of the Scriptures we might have hope and *overflow with confidence in His promises.*

ROMANS 15:4 AMP

The Bible is the best-selling book in history, but it is no ordinary book.
The words within its pages are life to your soul.

The precepts of the LORD are right, bringing joy to the heart;
The commandment of the LORD is pure, enlightening the eyes.

PSALM 19:8 AMP

Good friendships and healthy relationships make a major difference in each day—they make life a joy.

Perfume and incense bring joy to the heart, and the pleasantness of a friend springs from their heartfelt advice.

PROVERBS 27:9 NIV

What we put into our spirits will always affect how we live.

Guard your heart above all else, for it determines the course of your life.

PROVERBS 4:23 NLT

The most important relationship you will ever have is your relationship with God. Your relationship with Him is the foundation for every other relationship you will have.

"Love the Lord your God with all your passion and prayer and intelligence." This is the most important.... But there is a second to set alongside it: "Love others as well as you love yourself."

MATTHEW 22:37–39 MSG

Think of all God has done for you—He has saved you, He's delivered you, He has pulled you through times you never thought you could survive, and He loves you unconditionally.

In every situation [no matter what the circumstances] be thankful and *continually give thanks* to God, *for this is the will of God for you in Christ Jesus.*

1 Thessalonians 5:18 AMP

Remember that the happiest people are not those getting more, but those giving more.

H. Jackson Brown Jr.

Do you want to stand out? Then step down. Be a servant....
If you're content to simply be yourself, your life will count for plenty.

MATTHEW 23:11–12 MSG

When you truly love a person, you are willing to sacrifice anything for them.... Love is sacrifice, and sacrifice is love.

This is real love—not that we loved God, but that he loved us and sent his Son as a sacrifice to take away our sins. Dear friends, since God loved us that much, we surely ought to love each other.

1 John 4:10–11 NLT

One of the best, most joyful, most rewarding things you'll ever do in life is make a personal sacrifice in order to enrich someone else's life.

Do not forget to do good and to share with others, for with such sacrifices God is pleased.

HEBREWS 13:16 NIV

It is in selflessness that we find true peace and contentment.

If you have any encouragement from being united with Christ...then make my joy complete by being like-minded.... Do nothing out of selfish ambition or vain conceit. Rather, in humility value others above yourselves.

PHILIPPIANS 2:1–3 NIV

You can never out-give God—the more you seek to bless His people, the more He blesses you in return.

Live out your God-created identity. Live generously and graciously toward others, the way God lives toward you.

MATTHEW 5:48 MSG

Each new day is more than just another day of the week;
it's a new opportunity, a new beginning,
and you can live with an attitude of expectation.

My soul, wait silently for God alone, for my expectation is from Him.

Psalm 62:5 NKJV

JOYCE MEYER MINISTRIES
US AND FOREIGN OFFICE ADDRESSES

Joyce Meyer Ministries
P.O. Box 655
Fenton, MO 63026 USA
(636) 349-0303

Joyce Meyer Ministries—Canada
P.O. Box 7700
Vancouver, BC V6B 4E2 Canada
(800) 868-1002

Joyce Meyer Ministries—Australia
Locked Bag 77
Mansfield Delivery Centre
Queensland 4122 Australia
(07) 3349 1200

Joyce Meyer Ministries—England
P.O. Box 1549
Windsor SL4 1GT United Kingdom
01753 831102

Joyce Meyer Ministries—South Africa
P.O. Box 5
Cape Town 8000 South Africa
(27) 21-701-1056

ABOUT THE AUTHOR

JOYCE MEYER is one of the world's leading practical Bible teachers. A *New York Times* bestselling author, Joyce's books have helped millions of people find hope and restoration through Jesus Christ. Joyce's programs, *Enjoying Everyday Life* and *Everyday Answers* with Joyce Meyer, air around the world on television, radio, and the Internet. Through Joyce Meyer Ministries, Joyce teaches internationally on a number of topics with a particular focus on how the Word of God applies to our everyday lives. Her candid communication style allows her to share openly and practically about her experiences so others can apply what she has learned to their lives.

Joyce has authored more than one hundred books, which have been translated into more than one hundred languages, and over 65 million of her books have been distributed worldwide. Bestsellers include *Power Thoughts; The Confident Woman; Look Great, Feel Great; Starting Your Day Right; Ending Your Day Right; Approval Addiction; How to Hear from God; Beauty for Ashes*; and *Battlefield of the Mind*.

Joyce's passion to help hurting people is foundational to the vision of Hand of Hope, the missions arm of Joyce Meyer Ministries. Hand of Hope provides worldwide humanitarian outreaches such as feeding programs, medical care, orphanages, disaster response, human trafficking intervention and rehabilitation, and much more—always sharing the love and gospel of Christ.

Be so busy
LOVING
your life that you have
NO TIME
for hate, fear, or regret.